Family Spir[it]

Pray Together

Loving God,
hear the prayer of
this family
gathered here
before you.
In joy and love
unite all families
wherever they may be.

Now We Know

Q. Who gives us the
gift of life?
A. God our Father
gives us the gift of life.

*Just as the branch
cannot bear fruit by
itself unless it abides
in the vine, neither can
you unless you abide
in me*
(John 15:4)

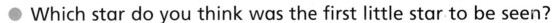

- Which star do you think was the first little star to be seen?
- Can you find some star families?
- What do the faces in the picture tell you about how they feel?
- How would these faces have looked before the stars came together in families?
- Can you draw a picture of sad stars and sad sun and moon?
- If you could be in this picture, what would you say to the stars, the sun and the moon?

Spirit of Friendship

Pray Together
May all of us who share your friendship be brought closer together in the unity of the Holy Spirit.

Now We Know
Q. Who gives us friends to love us?
A. God our Father gives us friends to love us.

Just as I have loved you, you also should love one another.
(John 13:34)

- Who can you see in this picture?
- What are they doing?
- Look at the bee's face – how do you think it is feeling right now?
- Which child do you think is Fiona?
- What would you say the children are talking about?
- Do you think these children are all friends?
- Why do you think so?
- If Fiona's bee could talk, what do you think it would say to the children?

- What is happening in this picture?
- Can you find the Queen Bee?
- Can you find the new bees?
- Do you think Fiona's bee is in this picture?
- Look at the flowers' faces – how do you think flowers feel about bees?
- What is the bees' home called?
- Where do bees store their honey?
- Can you draw a honeycomb pattern?

Earthed in the Spirit

Pray Together
Lord God, you are
wonderful indeed
And all creation rightly
gives you praise.
All life comes from you,
through your Son,
By the working of the
Holy Spirit.

*In his hand is the life
of every living thing
and the breath of
every human being.*
(Job 12:10)

Let us sing to the Lord :

Holy Spirit gather us round,

Make us one in mind and heart,

Through us, with us and in us.

The Spirit of God in David

Pray Together
Blessed are you
Lord God.

So all the elders of Israel came to the king at Hebron; and King David made a covenant with them at Hebron before the Lord, and they anointed David king over Israel.
(2 Samuel 5:3)

- Can you find David in the picture?
- What is David holding?
- Do you know of anyone else who carries a crook like David's?
- The children look happy – why is this a special day for them?
- Can you find the leaders of the twelve tribes?
- Are they all men? Why do you think the leaders are all men?
- Are all leaders today men?
- Can you think of a leader you know who is a woman?
- Who might the others in the picture be?
- Look at the sheep – what do you think is going on in their minds?
- What do you think the little girl on the right is doing?

The Feast of All Saints

Pray Together
St Brigid
Pray for us.
St Patrick
Pray for us.
St Colmcille
(also called
St Columba)
Pray for us.
St Margaret
Pray for us.

(You might
like to add
a local or
special saint
of your own.)

*To all God's beloved.
who are called to be
saints: Grace to you.*
(Romans 1:7)

- Which person is Mary Mary? Is this picture of her different from other nursery-rhyme pictures you've seen?
- Which are the wild flowers and which are the garden flowers?
- Do you recognise any of the flowers?
  – sunflower; buttercup; daisy etc.
- Make up names of your own for some of the flowers.
- Can you see the two little birds – what might they be saying to each other?

6

Eternal rest
grant unto them,
O Lord.
May they rest
in peace.

Praise to the Father,
Praise to the Son,
Praise to the Spirit,
The Three in One.

One day Jesus was walking by the shore of Lake Galilee. Simon (called Peter) and his brother Andrew were out in their boat, fishing. They were just about to throw their nets over the side when a voice called to them **'Come, follow me!'**

**Jesus – The One
Who Calls**

Pray Together
Jesus calls me,
I will go.
Jesus calls us.
Come, let us follow.

*And when day came,
he called his disciples
and chose twelve of
them...*
(Luke 6:13)

The two brothers looked up.
They saw Jesus on the shore.

'Come with me.
When you are fishing
you gather fish.
Now I am asking you
to gather people,' Jesus called.

They left their boats and nets
and followed him.

Jesus – Teaching and Nourishing

Pray Together
Jesus fed by
bread and word.
Jesus taught by
word and bread.
Jesus teach us;
Jesus feed us.
Living Bread;
Living Word.

Now when Jesus had finished saying these things, the crowds were astounded at his teaching...
(Matthew 7:28)

- Do you know what building this is? Does it remind you of anything?
- If you could go inside this building and look around, what do you think you would see and hear and smell?
- Who is inside the building?
- What is Jesus doing inside?
- Micah has dropped something – can you see what it is?
- Why do you think he dropped his money?

- Can you guess from the look on Micah's face what he is thinking about?
- How does Micah know that it is Jesus who is teaching inside the synagogue?
- How do you think Micah and Jesus would get along together?
- If you were in the picture instead of Micah, how would you and Jesus get along together?

Jesus – Saying and Doing

Pray Together

May all I say and do,
May all I do and say
Show your love,
Lord Jesus,
Every moment of
every day.

*I will show you what
someone is like
who comes to me,
hears my words,
and acts on them.*
(Luke 6:47)

'My name is Sayen; I talk a lot and I do nothing.'
'My name is Dooen; I do a lot but I say nothing.'
Dooen and Sayen jumped up and down with excitement.

They became close friends, talking and doing
things together.

Now they were very happy – and another
thing, instead of one being blue and the
other yellow, they had both turned into
wonderful shades of green! How do you
suppose that happened?

Jesus often said the word 'love'. How did he show what this word means? Let's look at our pictures and see if we can tell how Jesus put life into the word 'love'.

Now We Know
Q. Why did God our Father send his son, Jesus?
A. God our Father sent his son, Jesus, to tell us the Good News.

Q. What Good News did Jesus tell us?
A. Jesus told us that God our Father loves us and wants us to be his children.

Jesus told the crowds all these things in parables; without a parable he told them nothing.
(Matthew 13:34)

- How many things from the *Lost and Found* story can you find in this picture?
Now look at the pictures on the following two pages.
- What is the lamp saying to the woman?
- Look at the woman's face – can you tell how she is feeling?
- Who do you think is most helpful to the woman?
- Who is least helpful?
- What do you think makes some people helpful and some people unhelpful?
- What would you say to the people in the pictures?

One, two, three, four, five
Six, seven, eight, nine … drat!
There should be ten.
I've lost one coin.
Now how did I do that?

Where can it be?
Where has it gone?

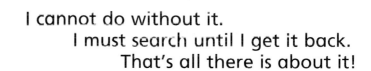

I cannot do without it.
I must search until I get it back.
That's all there is about it!

Jesus – Healing

Pray Together
Together with your child, say three Hail Marys for someone who is ill.

When Jesus entered Peter's house, he saw his mother-in-law lying in bed with a fever; he touched her hand, and the fever left her, and she got up and began to serve him.
(Matthew 8:14-15)

'Sarah!' he said gently. Sarah opened her eyes. The family were standing around her bed. Jesus was standing beside her, calling her name and holding her hand. Sarah smiled as Jesus helped her up out of bed and back onto her feet.

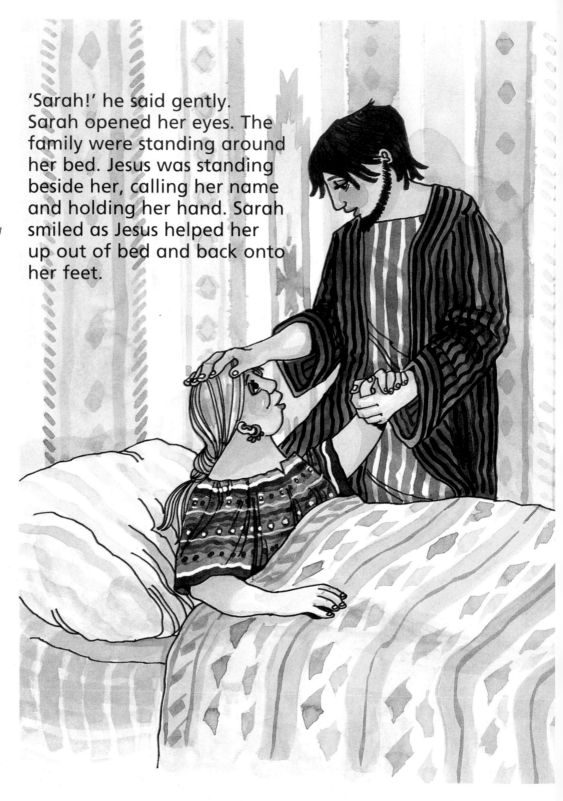

The People Who Walked In Darkness

Pray Together
Light an Advent Candle, preferably in a dark room. Hold your child's hand and sit quietly for a moment in its light.

The people who walked in darkness have seen a great light.
(Isaiah 9:2)

- What kind of a home do the wise men live in?
- If you could look around the rest of this tent, what other things would you expect to see?
- Why do you think there is a map and a pen on the floor?
- Do you think they are wise just to pack up and go? Why?

From Darkness To Light

Pray Together
The people who walked in darkness have seen a great light.
God, may your light shine on all who walk in darkness this night.

For we observed his star at its rising.
(Matthew 2:2)

- Where has the wise men's journey brought them to now?
- Would you like to ride on a camel?
- Who lives in this palace? Can you think of one word to describe Herod's palace?
- Look at Herod – what kind of person do you think he is?
- Do you think the wise men's journey will end here?
- Look at the wise men's faces – they are looking at Herod; what are they thinking?
- If you could be there with the wise men as they talk to Herod, what would you say to him?

Jesus – A Light For All

Pray Together
Blessed is the fruit of thy womb, Jesus.

Now We Know
Q. On what day was Jesus Christ, the Son of God, born?
A. Jesus Christ, the Son of God, was born on Christmas Day.

I am the light of the world. Whoever follows me will never walk in darkness but will have the light of life.
(John 8:12)

Joseph told the story of the angel's visit. Mary would have a baby. His name would be Immanu-El.

'Does that name have a meaning?' asked Balthasaar.

'It means "God is with us",' said Mary.

'Where or when or how is God with us?' Caspar asked.

Mary said, 'Right here and now, in the birth of my son, God is with us. In light and darkness, in sorrow and joy, in every moment of every day, God is with us.'

Balthasaar took the baby in his arms. 'Immanu-El, Immanu-El...' he began to sing.

Returning – A New Beginning

Pray Together

Goodbye to the
little cave.
Goodbye to the star.
Goodbye to the
wise men
Who journeyed so far.
Hello to a New Year.
Hello to each
new day.
Hello Hello
Emmanuel.
God's with us,
all the way.

*They worshipped him
and returned.*
(Luke 24:52)

- Where are the wise men going now?
- Look at their faces. How do you think they feel now tha[t]
  journey is over?
- Do you think there will be anyone in the tent to welcome
  home?
- Where might the star they followed be now?

22

- If you were one of the wise men, what's the first thing you'd do as soon as you got home?
- How would you explain to your family where you'd been?
- Do you think the wise men will ever see another bright star?
- Do you think they will ever go on another journey?

Being Me! Being Us!

Pray Together
Each moment,
Each hour
Of each and every day,
May we live in God
And God live in us.
Amen.

*You shall love
your neighbour
as yourself.*
(Matthew 22:39)

Us

I know a tiny little word –
It's small but it's fantastic.
It'll stretch to cover a multitude
Because it's made of elastic.

It stretches over families,
It covers neighbours and friends,
It fits all nations and peoples,
From here to the world's very end.

It stretches and stretches until –
Oh Dear! I fear it will burst!
But it doesn't. It snaps itself back
To its original – US!

Jairus' Daughter

Pray Together
Praise be to God
Always, everywhere.
Thanks be to God
Always, everywhere.
Glory be to God
Always, everywhere.

*Her spirit returned and
she got up at once.*
(Luke 8:55)

Now We Know
Q. When did we
become friends of
Jesus?
A. We became
friends of Jesus at
Baptism.

- These are two happy pictures – why are the people so happy?
- One picture shows Abigail as a baby – how old would you say she is?
- Who do you think the people outside the window are?
- Do you think the name 'Abigail' suits the baby?
- If you could choose another name, what would it be?
- If Jairus were to turn around and speak to the people at the window, what do you think he would say?

- Who is with Abigail in the second picture?
- What age do you think Abigail is now?
- Who are the people outside the window?
- Do you think Abigail knows who Jesus is?
- Do you think she and her friends might have heard of him or met him before?
- If you were one of Abigail's friends in this picture, what would you say to her?
- What would you say to Jesus?

MARINO INSTITUTE OF EDUCATION

Pray Together
Help us, O God,
this Lent
to remember
that we are
connected to you
each day.

*Then Jesus was led by
the Spirit into the
wilderness.*
(Matthew 4:1)

● What is happening in this picture?
● Have you ever taken part in something like this?
● Why are these children getting ashes on their foreheads?
● What might each of these children be thinking?
● Imagine some of these children are saying a prayer now – can you think what it might be?

The Good Shepherd

Pray Together
Act of Sorrow
O my God, I thank you
for loving me.
I am sorry for all my sins,
for not loving others
and not loving you.
Help me to live like Jesus
and not sin again. Amen.

*I am the Good Shepherd.
I know my own and my
own know me.*
(John 10:14)

● What is the shepherd holding in his hand? Why does a shepherd carry a crook?
● Have you ever seen anyone else carry a crook like this?
● The Good Shepherd knew every one of his sheep. He called each one by name. Can you think of names for all the sheep in the picture? (don't forget the lost sheep!)
● If you could be one of those sheep, which one would you like to be?
● When the lost sheep meets up with the rest of the flock again, what do you think it will say to them?
● Do you think the sheep at the bottom are looking at you? Perhaps they want to say something – what might it be?
● Have you anything to say to them?

Not Being Bothered, Not Being True

Pray Together
Prayer For Forgiveness
O my God, help me to remember the times when I didn't live as Jesus asked me to.
Help me to be sorry and to try again. Amen.

Now We Know
Q. What does the Lord Jesus ask his friends to do?
A. The Lord Jesus asks his friends to love God our Father and to love each other.

If we say that we have no sin, we deceive ourselves and the truth is not in us.
(1 John 1:8)

- What do you think is going on in this picture?
- Why do you think this is happening?
- Does what is going on here remind you of any time in your own life?
- What kinds of feelings do you think some people in this picture are having?
- Have you ever had feelings like these?

**Being a Bully,
Being Unfair,
Being Selfish**

Pray Together
Prayer After Forgiveness
O my God, thank you
for forgiving me.
Help me to love others.
Help me to live as Jesus
asked me to. Amen.

Now We Know
Q. What does God our
Father do for us in the
Sacrament of Penance?
A. In the Sacrament of
Penance, God our
Father forgives us.

*Be kind to one another,
tenderhearted,
forgiving one another,
as God in Christ has
forgiven you.*
(Ephesians 4:32)

- Do you think these children know any prayers?
- Can you think of any story which might be good for these children to hear?
- If you were in this picture, who do you think you would be?
- Who would you talk to?
- What would you say?
- Could you teach these children a prayer that you think might help them?

Pray Together

Jesus, remember me when you come into your Kingdom.

- What is going on in this picture?
- Who can you see?
- How do you think these people feel about Jesus?
- How do you think Jesus feels about them?
- If you could talk to these people, what would you say to them?
- If you could talk to Jesus, what would you say to him?

Now We Know

Q. What do we call the day on which Jesus died?
A. We call the day on which Jesus died Good Friday.

Q. What happened on Good Friday?
A. On Good Friday Jesus died on the cross.

Q. Why did Jesus die on the cross?
A. Jesus died on the cross to show his love for God the Father and for us.

Jesus, crying with a loud voice, said, 'Father, into your hands I commend my spirit'. Having said this he breathed his last.
(Luke 23:46)

31

The Resurrection

Now We Know

Q. What happened on
Easter Sunday?
A. On Easter Sunday
God the Father raised
Jesus from death to life
in a glorious body.

Q. Is the Lord Jesus still
with us?
A. Yes, the Lord Jesus is
still with us, for he said
'I am with you always'.

I have seen the Lord.
(John 20:18)

Simon Peter said to the others, 'I am going fishing.'
'We will come with you,' they told him.
So they went out in a boat and spent the night fishing, but they did not catch a thing.
As the sun was rising, Jesus stood at the water's edge, but the disciples did not know that it was Jesus. Then he asked them, 'Have you caught anything?'
'Not a thing,' they answered.
He said to them, 'Throw your net out on the right side of the boat, and you'll catch something.'
So they threw the net out and could not pull it in, because they had caught so many fish. Then John said to Peter, 'It is the Lord!'
(John 21:3-7)

Mary our Mother

Pray Together

Hail Mary, full of grace,
The Lord is with thee.
Blessed art thou
among women
And blessed is the fruit
of thy womb, Jesus.
Holy Mary,
Mother of God,
Pray for us sinners, now
And at the hour of
our death.
Amen.

*And blessed is she who
believed that there
would be a fulfilment
of what was spoken to
her by the Lord.*
(Luke 1:45)

Sing Together

At the cross her station keeping
Stood the blessed mother weeping,
Close to Jesus to the end.

Hour of darkness descending,
Mother, Son, love unending
On the hill of Calvary.

Mary, Mary crying.
Slowly Jesus dying.
Crucified, crucified.

Head bowed, body broken,
Breath breathed, last word
spoken,
'Abba, Father, Amen'.

33

**We Gather
Together
To Celebrate**

Pray Together
Blessed be God forever.

*For where two or three
are gathered in my
name, I am there
among them.
(Matthew 18:20)*

● Does this picture remind you of anything?
● Why are the people gathered together?
● What are the boy and girl going to do?
● What kind of clothes are they wearing?
● Do you know anyone who serves at Mass?
● What kind of clothes is the priest wearing?
● What do you notice about the way the people are dressed.

Pray Together
Open our ears, O Lord, that we may hear your word.

Now We Know
Q. What do we listen to at Mass?
A. At Mass we listen to the words of Jesus.

*The eyes of those who have sight will not be closed,
And the ears of those who have hearing will listen.*
(Isaiah 32:3)

Jairus and Hannah were really happy when their baby daughter was born. They called her Abigail. They watched with pride as she grew bigger, as she took her first step, as she said her first word, as she got taller and taller. They were pleased when she laughed and played with her friends. When she was happy, they were happy too.

Then one day when Abigail was twelve she stopped playing and laughing and crying and working and praying. She went into her room by herself. She lay on her bed. She closed her eyes. Jairus and Hannah knew that they must get help. Jairus went to Jesus and he said, 'Come quickly. Abigail needs you.' Jesus came. A neighbour said, 'You are too late'.

Jesus went into Abigail's room. He bent down and took her hand. He called her, 'Little girl, get up!' Hannah and Jairus watched in amazement as Abigail opened her eyes, smiled and got out of bed.

'God has done great things,' said Hannah.

'Holy is God's name,' Jairus replied.

We Celebrate Jesus' Love For Us

Pray Together
By your cross and resurrection you have set us free. You are the saviour of the world.

Now We Know
Q. What do we remember at Mass?
A. At Mass we remember Jesus' love for us.

As the father has loved me, so I have loved you; abide in my love.
(John 15:9)

- Can you find the sanctuary lamp and the crucifix on this page?
- We can see both of these in the church. Sometimes we see one of them in places other than a church – which one?
- Do you know anyone who has a crucifix in their home?
- Why do you think people sometimes have a crucifix in their home?
- What would it remind them of?
- What does the sanctuary lamp remind us of?

We Give Thanks

Pray Together

Lift up your hearts.
We lift them up to the Lord.

Let us give thanks to the Lord our God.
It is right to give thanks and praise.

Now We Know

Q. What do we do at Mass?

A. At Mass we praise and thank God our Father for Jesus.

Give thanks to the Lord for he is good.
(Psalm 106:1)

- ● Who is this man?
- ● Why are his bandages falling off?
- ● Look at his face – how do you think he is feeling?
- ● Who helped him to become well again?
- ● Where are the others whom Jesus helped?
- ● If you could talk to this man, what would you say to him?
- ● If you could talk to the others, what would you say to them?

We Celebrate God's Forgiveness

Pray Together
I confess to almighty God,
And to you, my brothers and sisters,
That I have sinned through my own fault,
In my thoughts and in my words,
In what I have done,
And in what I have failed to do;
And I ask blessed Mary, ever virgin,
All the angels and saints
And you, my brothers and sisters,
To pray for me to the Lord our God. Amen.

*Take heart, your
sins are forgiven.
(Matthew 9:2)*

- What are these children doing?
- How do you think they feel about what they are doing?
- Why are they doing this?
- Have you ever done this – when?
- Let's do it now…

We Share Jesus, The Bread Of Life

Pray Together
Christ has died.
Christ is risen.
Christ will come again.

Now We Know
Q. Who comes to us in Holy Communion?
A. The Lord Jesus comes to us in Holy Communion?
Q. Why does the Lord Jesus come to us in Holy Communion?
A. The Lord Jesus comes to us in Holy Communion to help us to love God our Father and to love one another.

At Mass
Christ is present in the
people gathered,
Christ is present in the
Gospel that's read,
Christ is present in the priest,
Christ is present in the
consecrated wine and bread.

This is the bread that came down from heaven. The one who eats this bread will live forever.
(John 6:58)

Go In Peace

Pray Together
Holy, holy, holy Lord,
God of power and might.
Heaven and earth are full
of your glory.
Hosanna in the highest.
Blessed is he who comes
in the name of the Lord.
Hosanna in the highest.

*Go in peace to love and
serve the Lord.*

Making PEACE

Making PEACE isn't easy!
I start it with P
For Patience with someone
Who's different to me.
Then E is for Everyone –
How can that be?
I've more than enough love
Inside me, you see.
And A is for Always,
Not just for today,
At home and at school
When I run out to play.
And C is for Caring,
That's doing what's good,
Not just when I have to
Or ought to, or should.
And E is for Ever
As Jesus has planned.
Oh, make PEACE in my heart, Lord,
And PEACE in our land.

The Spirit of God In Us

Pray Together

Holy Spirit,
Spirit of God,
Be our guide today.

Now We Know

Q. How does the Holy Spirit help us?
A. The Holy Spirit helps us to live like Jesus and to remember the words of Jesus.

Q. What do we call the friends of the Lord Jesus?
A. We call the friends of the Lord Jesus the Church.

Q. What do we celebrate when we are baptised?
A. When we are baptised we celebrate our sharing in the new life of the Lord Jesus.

If we live by the spirit, let us also be guided by the spirit.
(Galatians 5:25)

- Have you ever been to a Baptism?
- What do you remember about it?
- Do you know where you were baptised?
- Who are your godparents?
- Do you have your baptismal candle at home? Maybe you could look at it tonight!

The Spirit of God In Saint Gobnait

Pray Together

A Dhia na Cruinne,
Bí linn anseo.
Tabhair aire.
Bí a' faire
Anois 's go deo.
A Dhia, a bhronn orainn
Torthaí an tsaoil,
Bronn beannacht 's bua
Ar dheireadh mo scéal.

Good God, Almighty,
Be with us this day.
Protect us and save us
From harm and dismay.
Dear God, our Creator,
From whom good things come,
May our story end happily
Before this day is done.

(For use in Scotland)
A Dhia na Cruinne,
Bí cómhla ruinn an-diugh.
Thoir an aire.
Bí a' faire
A-nis 's gu tiugh.
A Dhia bhronn orainn
Toraidhean an t-saoghail,
Bronn beannacht 's buaidh
Orainn feasgair an-diugh.

Wait for the Lord;
be strong, and let your heart
take courage.
(Psalm 27:14)

One little bee – God bless it! –
Lit on the *Creachaire's nose –
Looked straight in his eye as if to say
'Right! This is as far as yis goes!'

*Cattle raider

42

These cattle belong to the people
Of Ballyvourney – they've little enough,
But we bees can give you
        "a little something" instead.'
Well! – that army just upped and ran off!

They took to their heels
        and ran for their life,
The *Beachaire Rua had won,
And unless I'm very much mistaken
They're probably still on the run.

*red-haired bee-keeper

Ballyvourney is free now! Ballyvourney is free
From the terrible Creachaire Crua.
Ballyvourney is free, thanks 🐝 to God
And the prayer of the Beachaire Rua.

Time To Go – Alive-O!

Pray Together

Being, belonging,
together as friends,
yeah, yeah! Alive-O!
Being, belonging,
beginning to end,
yeah, yeah! Alive-O!
Together as friends.

*O give thanks to the
Lord, for he is good;
for his steadfast love
endures for ever.
(Psalm 107:1)*

- Who do you see?
- Where have you
  seen them before?
- Can you remember
  the stories?
- Pick out your
  favourites...

45

The Sign of the Cross
In the name of the Father, and of the Son,
and of the Holy Spirit. Amen.

Glory be to the Father
Glory be to the Father,
and to the Son,
and to the Holy Spirit,
as it was in the beginning,
is now and ever shall be,
world without end. Amen.

Morning Prayer
Father in heaven, you love me,
you're with me night and day.
I want to love you always
in all I do and say.
I'll try to please you, Father.
Bless me through the day. Amen.

Night Prayer
God, our Father, I come to say
thank you for your love today.
Thank you for my family,
and all the friends you give to me.
Guard me in the dark of night,
and in the morning send your light. Amen.

Grace before Meals
Bless us, O God, as we sit together.
Bless the food we eat today.
Bless the hands that made the food.
Bless us, O God. Amen.

Grace after Meals
Thank you, God, for the food we have
eaten.
Thank you, God, for all our friends.
Thank you, God, for everything.
Thank you, God. Amen.

Journey Prayer
Arise with me in the morning.
Travel with me through each day.
Welcome me on my arrival.
God, be with me all the way.

Our Father
Our Father who art in heaven
hallowed be thy name.
Thy kingdom come,
thy will be done
on earth as it is in heaven.
Give us this day our daily bread
and forgive us our trespasses
as we forgive those who trespass against us
And lead us not into temptation.
But deliver us from evil. Amen.

Hail Mary
Hail Mary, full of grace,
the Lord is with thee.
Blessed art thou among women
and blessed is the fruit of thy womb, Jesus.
Holy Mary, mother of God,
pray for us sinners,
now, and at the hour of our death. Amen.

Prayer to Jesus
Christ be with me.
Christ be beside me.
Christ be before me.
Christ be behind me.
Christ at my right hand.
Christ at my left hand.
Christ be with me everywhere I go.
Christ be my friend, for ever and ever. Amen

Prayer to the Trinity
Praise to the Father.
Praise to the Son.
Praise to the Spirit.
The Three in One. Amen.

Prayers to Mary
Mary, mother of Jesus,
I want to live and love like you.
I want to love the Father,
I want to love like Jesus.

Mother of Jesus, blessed are you.
Mother of Jesus, my mother too.
Help me to live like Jesus
and help me to live like you.

Prayers to the Holy Spirit

Holy Spirit I want to do what is right.
Help me.
Holy Spirit I want to live like Jesus.
Guide me.
Holy Spirit I want to pray like Jesus.
Teach me.

Spirit of God in the heavens.
Spirit of God in the seas.
Spirit of God in the mountain tops.
Spirit of God in me.
Spirit of God in the sunlight.
Spirit of God in the air.
Spirit of God all around me.
Spirit of God everywhere.
Holy Spirit, Spirit of God, help me.

*Confiteor

I confess to almighty God,
and to you, my brothers and sisters,
that I have sinned through my own fault
in my thoughts and in my words,
in what I have done,
and in what I have failed to do;
and I ask blessed Mary, ever virgin,
all the angels and saints,
and you, my brothers and sisters,
to pray for me to the Lord our God.

*Act of Sorrow

O my God,
I thank you for loving me.
I am sorry for all my sins, for not loving
others and not loving you.
Help me to live like Jesus and not sin
again. Amen.

*Prayer for Forgiveness

O my God,
help me to remember the times when I
didn't live as Jesus asked me to.
Help me to be sorry and to try again.
Amen.

*Prayer after Forgiveness

O my God,
thank you for forgiving me.
Help me to love others.
Help me to live as Jesus asked me to.
Amen.

*Prayer before Communion

Lord Jesus, come to me.
Lord Jesus, give me your love.
Lord Jesus, come to me and give me
yourself.

Lord Jesus, friend of children, come to me.
Lord Jesus, you are my Lord and my God.
Praise to you, Lord Jesus Christ.

*Prayer after Communion

Lord Jesus, I love and adore you.
You're a special friend to me.
Welcome, Lord Jesus, O welcome,
thank you for coming to me.

Thank you, Lord Jesus, O thank you
for giving yourself to me.
Make me strong to show your love
wherever I may be.

Be near me, Lord Jesus, I ask you to stay
close by me forever and love me, I pray.
Bless all of us children in your loving care
and bring us to heaven to live with you
there.

I'm ready now, Lord Jesus.
To show how much I care.
I'm ready now to give your love
at home and everywhere.

*These prayers are particularly relevant
to those children preparing for
First Communion and First Penance.*

The Children of God Series

Third Presentation
Series Director: Maura Hyland
Writing Team: Eleanor Gormally, Maura Hyland and Clare Maloney

First published 1999 by
Veritas Publications, 7/8 Lower Abbey Street, Dublin 1

ISBN 1 85390 480 5

Art Director: Bill Bolger
Illustrations: Jeanette Dunne
Poem on page 40 by Christy Kenneally
Origination: Accuplate Ltd
Printed in Ireland by Smurfit Web Press